CARROTS THE BUNNY

Model Magic®: white, green, orange, pink (red + white) basic supplies (see inside the front cover)

1 Body: Flatten a $1^1/2$" white ball on the bottom. **Feet**: Shape two $7/8$" white balls into pears. Attach to the body bottom. Use the knife to draw toes in the large ends. Attach three flattened pink balls onto each foot. **Arms**:

Flatten two $3/4$" white balls into pears. Attach to the shoulders and curve the arms to touch the tops of the feet.

2 Head: Roll a $1^1/8$" ball of white. Flatten two small white balls side by side on the front for the muzzle. Press a pink ball onto the muzzle top. **Ears**: Flatten two $1/2$" white balls into teardrops. Attach the points to the head. Bend the rounded ends forward.

3 Carrot: Roll a $2^1/2$" long orange cone. Use the knife to draw the lines around it. Flatten two $1/2$" green balls into ovals. Use the knife to draw leaf veins. Attach them to the top of the carrot. Press the carrot into the bunny's arms as shown in the large photo. Let the bunny dry, then use the pen to dot his eyes and whiskers.

TIM TURTLE

Model Magic®: yellow, green, white basic supplies (see inside the front cover)

1 Shell: Shape a 2" yellow ball into a dome. Wrap a $1/4$"x$6^1/2$" green rope around the bottom. **Feet**: Flatten four $3/4$" balls and set them $3/4$" apart in a square. Place the shell on the feet. Use the knife to draw toes.

2 Tail: Roll a $1/2$" long green teardrop. Attach the round end under the shell back and curve the point up. **Spots**: Flatten several green balls and attach them evenly spaced over the shell top. Flatten some small yellow balls and press onto the green spots. Flatten four small green balls and attach around the lower area of the shell.

3 Head and neck: Roll a $2^1/4$" long green teardrop. Attach the point under the shell front. Curve the neck and head up in an S. Use the knife to draw a mouth. Attach two $1/2$" green balls side by side on top of the head. Indent the fronts with your little finger. Press small white balls into the fronts. After the turtle is dry, use the black pen to draw pupils.

back view

COWBOY DAN

Model Magic®: white, black, blue, red, brown (red + green), pink (red + white) tracing paper, pencil, basic supplies (see inside the front cover)

1 **Boots**: Roll two 1" long black eggs. Place the round ends together. **Jeans**: Shape a ¹/₂"x4" blue log into a U. Attach the ends to the boots. **Shirt**: Attach a 1¹/₂" wide white oval to the jeans. **Arms**: Roll two ¹/₂"x2" white logs. Attach to the shoulders and curve down. Attach ¹/₂" pink balls for hands.

2 **Bandana**: Flatten red clay very flat. Trace the bandana onto tracing paper and cut out. Lay on the clay and cut around it. Drape it around his neck with the ends touching in back.

bandana

3 **Head**: Attach a 1" pink ball to the top. Attach a small pink ball for a nose. Shape two ³/₄" long black teardrops. Place points out below the nose. Curl the points outward.

4 Flatten a 1" black ball for the hat brim. Attach a 1" black ball on top. Indent the top with the side of a toothpick. Curve the brim up to touch the top and put on his head. **Rope**: Coil a ¹/₄"x4" brown rope. Place it under his right hand. Let dry. Use a black pen to dot eyes and draw eyebrows. Draw a zig-zag along the bandana edge and dots between the points.

HANK THE HORSE

Model Magic®: white, brown (red + green) ball-headed pin (to indent nostrils) basic supplies (see inside the front cover)

1 **Legs**: Shape four 1" tall white cones. Flatten a brown ball on the bottom of each. Place the legs together. **Body**: Roll a 1"x1¹/₂" white oval and attach to the legs. Flatten small brown balls and attach to his rump. **Head**: Shape a 1" long white teardrop. Pinch the small end to shape the nose. Use the knife to draw his mouth and the pin head to indent nostrils. Attach to the top front of the body, nose angled up.

2 **Ears**: Flatten two ¹/₄" white balls into teardrops. Attach to the head, leaving a space for the mane. **Mane**: Flatten a ¹/₄"x1¹/₂" brown log. Use the knife to draw hair lines. Attach to the neck back and between the ears. **Tail**: Roll a 1¹/₂" tall brown cone. Use the knife to draw hair lines. Attach the point to his rump and curve the tail down to touch the body. Pinch the bottom up. After he is dry, use the pen to dot eyes.

2

LOVEY LAMB

Model Magic®: black, white
basic supplies (see inside the
front cover)

1 **Feet**: Slightly flatten four
¹/₂" black balls and place
them together in a square.

Body: Roll
a 1¹/₄" long
white oval.
Attach to
the tops of
the feet.
Head: Press
a 1" long
black egg
onto the body front with the
small end extending upward.
Use the knife to draw the
muzzle.

muzzle

2 Flatten two ¹/₄" black balls
into teardrops and attach
to the sides of the head.
Flatten many ¹/₈"–¹/₄" white
balls and attach all over the
body and neck area for wool.

PINKY PIG

pink Model Magic® (red + white)
ball-headed pin (to indent nostrils)
basic supplies (see inside the
front cover)

1 **Legs**: Shape four ¹/₂" tall
cones. Press the points
together. **Body**: Attach a 1" ball
on top of the legs. **Head**: Roll a
³/₄" ball and press onto the top
front of the body.

2 **Ears**: Flatten
two ¹/₂" balls into
diamonds. Attach to
the top of the head, ¹/₄" apart.
Flatten a ³/₈" ball onto the
front of the head. Indent
nostrils with the pin head. Roll a
¹/₈"x³/₄" rope, coil and attach to
the rump. After the pig is dry,
use the pen to dot eyes.

**pig
ear**

SPOT THE COW

Model Magic®: black, white, brown (red + green),
pink (red + white)
ball-headed pin (to indent nostrils)
basic supplies (see inside the front cover)

1 **Legs**: Shape four 1" tall white cones.
Flatten a brown ball on the bottom
of each. Use the knife to draw a line
on the front of each hoof. Place the legs
together. **Body**: Roll a 1"x1¹/₂" white oval
and attach to the legs.

2 **Head**: Attach a 1¹/₄" white ball to the
top front of the body. Slightly flatten
the lower part. Flatten a 1" wide pink
oval and attach to the center. Roll a short
pink rope for a chin. Use the pin head to
indent nostrils.

3 **Horns**: Shape two ¹/₄" tall brown
cones. Attach to the top of her head.
Ears: Flatten two ¹/₂" black balls into
ovals. Attach one on each side of the
horns, extending outward. **Tail**: Roll a
2" long white teardrop. Flatten the large
end and pinch into a point. Use the
knife to draw hair lines. Bend into an
S and attach to her rump as shown.
Spots: Flatten many small black balls
and attach all over her body and legs.
After she's dry, use the pen to dot eyes.

HEN & CHICKS

Model Magic®: white, yellow, red, orange
basic supplies (see inside the front cover)

1 **Hen**: Roll a 1 1/4" ball of white into an oval. On one end, pinch up a tail. Roll a 1/2" white ball and attach for the head.

2 Flatten two 3/4" white balls into teardrops and attach one on each side for wings. Tip the ends upward. Use the knife to draw feather lines on the wing tips and tail. Roll three small red balls and attach as shown for the comb. Shape a yellow cone and attach for the beak. Make a red teardrop and attach below the beak for the wattle.

3 **Chick**: Roll a 3/8" yellow ball into a teardrop. Tip the tail up. Attach a yellow ball for the head. Shape a tiny orange cone for the beak. Make as many chicks as you want. When the hen and chicks are dry, use the black pen to dot eyes.

DUCK FAMILY

Model Magic®: white, yellow, orange
basic supplies (see inside the front cover)

mama duck's foot

◆ **duckling's foot**

1 **Mama duck**: Roll a 1" white ball for the body. Flatten a 1/2" white ball into a teardrop. Attach the point to the ball bottom and tip up for a tail. Flatten two 3/4" white balls into teardrops and attach for wings. Use the knife to draw feather lines on the wings and tail. Attach a white ball for the head. Shape two 3/8" orange balls into teardrops. Flatten slightly and press the points together. Cut the points off. Attach the cut end to her face. Flatten two 1/2" orange balls into diamonds and attach for feet.

back view

2 **Duckling**: Shape as for the mama duck, but use a 1/2" yellow ball for the body and pinch up to form the tail. Use yellow for the head and wings. Use orange for the bills and feet. Make as many ducklings as you want. When the mama and ducklings are dry, use the black pen to dot eyes.

THREE BEARS + ONE

Model Magic®: black, blue, yellow, green, red
basic supplies (see inside the front cover)

1 **Blue bear**: Shape a 1 1/2" blue ball into an egg. Roll two 2" long blue teardrops for legs. Attach the small ends under his bottom, angled apart. Use your thumb to push up toes. Roll two 5/8"x1" blue logs for arms. Pinch one end of each to a flattened point and attach at the top of the body. Curve the arms forward around his tummy.

2 Slightly flatten a 1" blue ball and attach for his head. Slightly flatten a blue oval and attach to the bottom front of the head. Use your finger to indent the center top. Roll a black ball and attach for the nose. Use your little finger to flatten and indent two 1/4" blue balls and attach for ears. After the bear is dry, use the black pen to dot eyes.

3 **Other bears**: Follow steps 1–2, but use different solid or marbled colors. The arms can extend outward or upward instead of curving over the tummy.

CUDDLE KITTIES

Model Magic®: white, black, pink (red + white)
white acrylic paint or paint pen
basic supplies (see inside the front cover)

1 **White kitty's body**: Roll a 2" tall white teardrop. Use a knife to indent a 1" long line at the bottom front. **Feet**: Attach four 3/4" white balls as shown. Use the knife to draw toes. **Head**: Attach a 1" white ball to the body top. Slightly flatten two small white balls side by side for a muzzle. Attach a pink ball for a nose and a pink oval for a tongue. Pinch two 1/4" tall white cones for ears. **Tail**: Attach one end of a 1/2"x2 1/2" white rope to the bottom back. Curve it over the hip. After the kitty dries, use the black pen to dot eyes and whiskers.

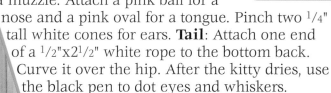
top view

2 **Black kitty**: Follow step 1, but use black for the body, head and ears. Before indenting the body, press flattened white clay onto the bottom front. Press a 1/2" white ball onto one side of a 3/4" black ball and roll together for the tail.

back view

FREDDY FIREDOG

Model Magic®: red, white, blue, black
ball-headed pin (to indent nozzle)
basic supplies (see inside the front
cover)

back view

1 **Feet**: Roll two 1" black balls into ovals and flatten the backs. Set so the toes angle apart. **Tail**: Attach a 1/4" black ball to one side of a 1/2" white ball. Roll into a 1 1/2" long teardrop. Place the large end behind the feet and curve the tip up. **Coat**: Shape a 2" tall red cone. Attach over the feet and tail. Use the knife to draw a line down the front.

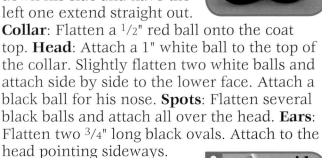

2 **Arms**: Roll two 1 1/4" long red teardrops. Attach the small ends to the top of the coat. Attach a white ball to the end of each arm. Let the right arm hang down his side and have the left one extend straight out. **Collar**: Flatten a 1/2" red ball onto the coat top. **Head**: Attach a 1" white ball to the top of the collar. Slightly flatten two white balls and attach side by side to the lower face. Attach a black ball for his nose. **Spots**: Flatten several black balls and attach all over the head. **Ears**: Flatten two 3/4" long black ovals. Attach to the head pointing sideways.

3 **Helmet**: Flatten a 1" red ball into a 2 1/2" long teardrop. Attach so the round end extends over the face. Roll a 1" red ball into a teardrop and press onto the brim with the front over the face.

side view

Flatten a white cone onto the helmet front. **Hose**: Roll a 1/4"x9" blue log. Attach to the hands as shown. Flatten a black ball onto one end. Attach a black cone, then a smaller black ball. Use the pin head to indent it. After the dog is dry, use the black pen to dot eyes and whiskers. Write "1" on the front of the helmet. Draw three toggles ▭ on his coat front.

YELLOW DOG

Model Magic®: yellow, blue, red, black
basic supplies (see inside the front cover)

1 **Feet**: Roll two 1" yellow balls into ovals and flatten the backs. Use the knife to draw toes. Attach so the toes angle apart. **Body**: Roll a 1 1/2" tall yellow cone. Press onto the feet. **Front paws**: Shape two 1" yellow balls into teardrops and flatten slightly. Attach as shown.

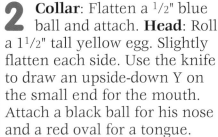

2 **Collar**: Flatten a 1/2" blue ball and attach. **Head**: Roll a 1 1/2" tall yellow egg. Slightly flatten each side. Use the knife to draw an upside-down Y on the small end for the mouth. Attach a black ball for his nose and a red oval for a tongue.

3 **Ears**: Flatten two 1/2" yellow balls into teardrops. Attach the round ends to his head. Curl the points forward to touch the face. **Tail**: Roll a 1 1/2" long yellow teardrop. Attach the round end to his rump and curve the tail to one side. After the dog is dry, use the black pen to dot eyes and whiskers.

back view

BULLDOG BILL

*Model Magic®: blue, white, black
basic supplies (see inside the
front cover)*

1 **Body**: Roll a 2" long blue oval. Flatten the sides slightly. **Legs**: Shape four 1¼" long blue eggs. Flatten the large ends and bend the small

ends forward. Use the knife to draw toes. Attach as shown— the body shouldn't touch the ground.

Tail: Shape a ³/₈" long blue cone. Attach to his rump and turn the tip up.

2 **Head**: Slightly flatten a 1¼" blue ball. Use your thumb to indent the bottom. Flatten and shape a ¾" blue ball the same way and attach

to the lower face. Flatten and shape a smaller blue ball the same way and attach to the last one for the chin. Use your little finger to indent the center ball top. Attach a black ball for his nose.

3 **Eyes**: Attach a white ball on each side of the nose. Wrap a ¼"x1" blue log around the top of each eye, pushing the inner ends together. **Ears**: Flatten two 1" long blue teardrops. Attach the large ends to the head. Tip the points forward to touch the eyebrows. After he's dry, use the black pen to draw his pupils and dot whiskers.

OSKAR THE WIENER DOGGY

*Model Magic®: red, white, black
basic supplies (see inside the front cover)*

1 **Body**: Roll a ¾"x3" red log. Bend it slightly at the center to make a sway back. **Feet**: Roll four ⁵/₈" long red eggs. Attach two under the body front, small ends together. Bend up the small ends of the others and attach under the body back, large ends to the sides. Use the knife to draw toes.

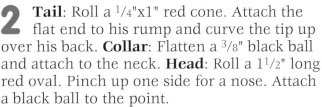

2 **Tail**: Roll a ¼"x1" red cone. Attach the flat end to his rump and curve the tip up over his back. **Collar**: Flatten a ³/₈" black ball and attach to the neck. **Head**: Roll a 1½" long red oval. Pinch up one side for a nose. Attach a black ball to the point.

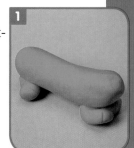

3 **Ears**: Flatten two ³/₈" red balls into eggs. Attach to the sides of the head, small ends up. **Eyes**: Roll two ³/₈" red balls. Flatten slightly, then pinch one side of each to flatten it more. Attach between the ears, with the flattened sides to the front. Press a white ball onto the front of each eye. Flatten two tiny black balls and attach to the whites for pupils. When the doggy is dry, use the black pen to dot his whiskers.

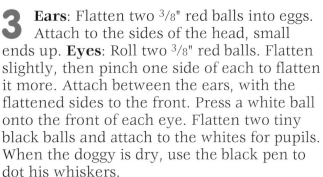

RONNI RHINO

orange Model Magic®
ball-headed pin (to indent ears)
basic supplies (see inside the front cover)

1 **Legs**: Flatten four ³/₈" orange balls and place in a square. Flatten a smaller orange ball on top of each. **Body**: Roll a 1¹/₂" long orange oval. Press onto the legs. **Tail**: Roll a ¹/₈"x¹/₂" orange rope and attach to her rump. Tip the end up.

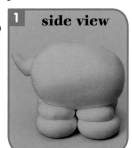

1 side view

2 **Head**: Roll a 1" long orange oval. Pinch one end upward into a point for a nose. Attach the bottom back to the body. Shape a ¹/₂" tall orange cone and attach it to the nose point. Curve the tip back slightly. **Ears**: Roll two ¹/₄" orange balls. Indent the front of each with the pin head, then attach them to the head. After she's dry, use the black pen to dot her eyes.

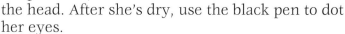

2

HANSI HIPPO

green Model Magic®
ball-headed pin (to indent ears & nostrils)
basic supplies (see inside the front cover)

1 **Legs**: Flatten four ³/₈" green balls and place in a square. Flatten a smaller green ball on top of each (see Ronni's photo). **Body**: Roll a 1¹/₂" long green oval. Flatten the top and bottom slightly and press onto the legs. **Tail**: Roll a ¹/₈"x¹/₂" green rope and attach to her rump. Tip the end up.

2 **Head**: Roll a 1" wide green oval. Roll a smaller green ball into an oval and press onto the first. Place the head on the top front of the body with the large oval forward. Use the pin to indent nostrils as shown. Roll a ¹/₈"x⁵/₈" green rope and attach to the bottom front for the mouth. **Ears**: Roll

2

two ¹/₄" green balls. Indent the front of each with the pin head, then attach to the top of the head. After she's dry, use the black pen to dot her eyes.

ELLI PHANT

blue Model Magic®
basic supplies (see inside the front cover)

1 **Legs**: Flatten four ¹/₂" blue balls and place in a square. Flatten a smaller blue ball on top of each (see Ronni's photo). **Body**: Roll a 1³/₄" blue ball into an oval. Flatten the sides slightly and attach to the legs. **Tail**: Roll a ¹/₈"x¹/₂" blue rope and attach to her rump. Tip the end up.

2 **Head**: Attach a ³/₄" blue ball to the body front. **Ears**: Flatten two 1" long blue ovals. Pinch the side of one and attach to her head. Repeat on the other side of her head. The ears should stick straight out. **Trunk**: Roll six ¹/₄"–³/₈" blue balls and flatten each. Stack in size order and attach the large end to her head. Curve the trunk up. After she's dry, use the black pen to dot her eyes.

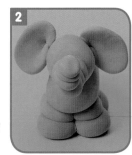

2

ZEKE ZEBRA

Model Magic®: black, white
basic supplies (see inside
the front cover)

1 Marble black and white clay (see inside the front cover). Use this for all the pieces. **Legs**: Slightly flatten four ³/₄" balls and place in a square. Slightly flatten a smaller ball on top of each. **Body**: Roll a 1"x1¹/₂" oval and attach to the tops of the legs.

2 **Head**: Slightly flatten a ¹/₂" ball and attach for the neck. Shape a 1" long egg. Attach the large end to the neck and bend the small end up slightly. **Ears**: Flatten two ¹/₂" long teardrops. Attach to the head, leaving an opening for the mane.

3 **Mane**: Flatten a ¹/₄"x1¹/₂" long log. Use the knife to draw hair. Attach to the neck, extending forward between the ears. **Tail**: Roll a ¹/₈"x1" rope and flatten one end. Use the knife to draw hair lines in the flat end. Attach the small end to his rump. After he's dry, use the black pen to dot his eyes.

back view

GEORGIA GIRAFFE

Model Magic®: yellow, orange
basic supplies (see inside the front cover)

1 **Body**: Roll a 1"x1¹/₂" yellow oval. **Legs**: Slightly flatten four ⁵/₈" yellow balls. Stack two smaller yellow balls on each. Attach two in the front and two in back. **Neck**: (Be sure to use toothpicks to reinforce the neck and head.) Slightly flatten a ³/₄" yellow ball and attach at the top front of the body. Slightly flatten four smaller yellow balls and stack them on the first one, angling the stack slightly forward.

2 **Head**: Roll a 1" long yellow oval and attach to the neck. **Horns**: Shape two ¹/₄" yellow balls into teardrops. Roll the small ends between your thumb and forefinger to make a club shape. Attach to the back of the head. **Ears**: Flatten two ¹/₄" long yellow ovals. Attach one behind and outside of each horn.

3 **Tail**: Roll a ¹/₈"x³/₄" yellow rope and flatten one end. Use the knife to draw hair lines in the flat end. Attach the small end to her rump. **Spots**: Roll many small orange balls, flatten and press onto the neck and body. After she's dry, use the black pen to dot her eyes.

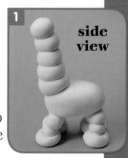

side view

back view

PIPER PENGUIN

Model Magic®: black, white, orange
white acrylic paint or paint pen
basic supplies (see inside the front cover)

1 **Feet**: Shape two 1" long orange teardrops. Flatten the points. Place side by side with the toes angled apart. Use the knife to draw toes. **Body**: Shape a 2" tall black egg. Flatten a 1" white oval, flatten onto the lower front. Set the body on the feet.

2 **Beak**: Flatten two 1/2" orange triangles. Attach one on top of the other. Attach the joined end at the top of the tummy. **Wings**: Flatten two 3/4" tall black teardrops. Attach the round ends to the sides near the top of the tummy. Curve the tips outward. After he's dry, use a toothpick to dot on white paint for eyes.

beak

side view

BAILEY WHALE

Model Magic®: blue, black, white
ball-headed pin (to indent the blowhole)
basic supplies (see inside the front cover)

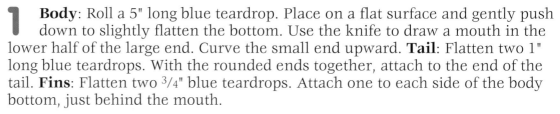

1 **Body**: Roll a 5" long blue teardrop. Place on a flat surface and gently push down to slightly flatten the bottom. Use the knife to draw a mouth in the lower half of the large end. Curve the small end upward. **Tail**: Flatten two 1" long blue teardrops. With the rounded ends together, attach to the end of the tail. **Fins**: Flatten two 3/4" blue teardrops. Attach one to each side of the body bottom, just behind the mouth.

2 **Eyes**: Roll two 1/4" black balls. Flatten two 1/8" blue balls into 1/2" long ovals. Wrap one oval over the top of each eye, then press an eye onto each side of the head above the corners of the mouth. **Blowhole**: Roll a 3/8" blue ball and attach to the top of the head. Use the pin head to indent the center.

3 **Spout**: Marble (see inside the front cover) blue and white clay. Roll the marbled clay into three 1/4"x3" ropes. Place them side by side and twist the ends together. Roll the twisted ends to smooth them. Curl the other ends into spirals as shown. Let the spout and whale dry separately. After they're dry, glue the spout into the blowhole.

WINSTON WALRUS

Model Magic®: blue, white, black
basic supplies (see inside the front cover)

1 **Body**: Shape a 3" long blue teardrop. Flatten the pointed end and use a knife to cut a 1" slit in the point, then pull the ends apart to form flippers. Tip the round end up for the head.

2 **Front flippers**: Flatten two ¹/₂" long blue teardrops. Attach the round ends under the body where it curves off the table. Bend the points out to support the front.

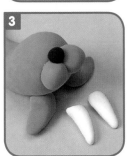

3 **Muzzle**: Attach two ¹/₂" blue balls to the front of the head. Attach a black ball for a nose. Shape two 1" long white cones. Attach the flat ends to the bottom of the muzzle. After he's dry, use the black pen to dot his eyes and whiskers.

ROLEY POLAR BEAR

Model Magic®: white, black
ball-headed pin (to indent ears)
basic supplies (see inside the front cover)

1 **Body**: Shape a 2" tall white egg, 1" thick. Stand it small end up. **Back feet**: Roll two 1" long white eggs. Flatten the small ends and attach them under the sides.

2 **Front feet**: Flatten two ³/₄" white balls and attach as shown. Use the knife to draw toes in all four feet. **Head**: Shape a 1¹/₄" tall white egg and flatten slightly. Attach to the body front, small end down, right on top of the front feet. Attach a black ball to the bottom for his nose.

3 **Ears**: Roll two ¹/₄" white balls and use the head of the pin to indent the fronts. Attach them to the top of the head. **Tail**: Roll a ¹/₂" long white teardrop and attach to his rump. After he's dry, use the black pen to dot his eyes.

side view

STAR & STARLET

Model Magic®: orange, yellow, white, black ball-headed pin (to indent spots and mouth) basic supplies (see inside the front cover)

1 **Star**: Shape five 2¹/₂" long orange cones. Attach as shown to form a star. Press a ¹/₂" orange ball into the bottom center area and indent it with the pin head for a mouth. Attach two ³/₈" white balls above the mouth for

eyes. Attach two smaller black balls for pupils. Press many small yellow balls onto each arm and indent each.

2 **Starlet**: Follow step 1, but make 2" long cones. Use a ¹/₄" orange ball for the mouth and leave out the eyes.

tail

claw

LYLE LOBSTER

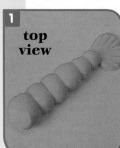
top view

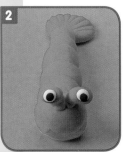

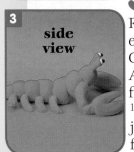
side view

Model Magic®: red, white, black ball-headed pin (to indent eyes) basic supplies (see inside the front cover)

1 **Body**: Roll six 1¹/₄"–¹/₂" red balls. Press them together in size order. **Tail**: Flatten a ⁷/₈" red ball into a fan. Use the knife to draw spines. Attach the point to the small end of the body.

2 **Head**: Roll a ³/₄" red ball and attach to the top front. **Eyes**: Shape two ¹/₂" long red cones. Place the points side by side on the head. Curve the flat ends apart and indent with your little finger. Roll two ¹/₄" white balls and attach one to the end of each cone. Use the pin head to indent them. Attach black balls for pupils.

3 **Claws**: Roll two 1" long red eggs. Slightly flatten the large ends and attach to the shoulders below the head. Roll two ³/₈"x¹/₂" red logs and attach to the bottoms of the eggs, extending forward. Flatten two 1" red balls into ovals. Cut 1" into one end of each and spread the cut ends apart. Attach the round ends to the red logs, bending the claws in front of the body. **Legs**: Roll eight ³/₄" long red ovals and cut ¹/₂" into one end of each. Attach the round ends between the joints of the body, four on each side. Curve each leg slightly forward.

SEELY SEAHORSE

Model Magic®: red, black
ball-headed pin (to indent nose & eye)
basic supplies (see inside the front cover)

 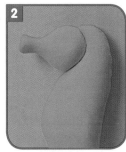

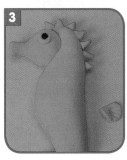

1 **Body**: Shape a 4" long red oval. Roll one end into a point and curve it into a backward C—this is where the head will fit. Roll the other end into a longer point. Curve it forward into a spiral to make the tail.

2 **Head**: Flatten a 1" ball into a teardrop. Pinch and roll the small end to make a "handle" shape for the nose. Flatten the end of the nose and indent with the pin head. Attach it in the top curve of the body.

3 **Eye**: Roll a 1/4" red ball. Attach to the side of the head and indent with the pin head. Roll a black ball and place in the indentation. **Mane**: Shape seven 1/4" red cones and attach in a row over the top of the head and down the back of the neck. **Fin**: Flatten a 3/8" long red teardrop. Draw spines with the knife. Attach the point to his side and bend the round end forward.

CONNIE CRAB

Model Magic®: blue, white, black
basic supplies (see inside the front cover)

1 **Body**: Shape a 1 1/2"x2" blue dome. **Eyes**: Attach two 1/2" blue balls to the top, just in front of the center. Use your little finger to indent the fronts. Attach white balls to the fronts and black balls for the pupils.

claw

2 **Claws**: Roll two 1/2"x1" blue logs. Attach them to the front of the body. Flatten two 1 1/2" long blue ovals. Cut 1" into one end of each and spread the cut ends apart. Smooth and round the cut areas. Attach the claws to the blue logs.

3 **Legs**: Roll eight 3/8"x3/4" logs. Attach four equally spaced along each side of the body. Roll eight 5/8" long blue cones. Attach the flat end of each cone to the end of a log. Curve the tips toward the front.

BUMBLE BUG

Model Magic®: yellow, black
basic supplies (see inside the front cover)

1 Body: Roll four ¹/₂" yellow balls and four ¹/₂" black balls. Flatten and stack them, alternating colors. Roll another yellow ball and place on the black end. Roll a ³/₈" long black cone and place on the top back of the last yellow ball for a stinger.

2 Head: Roll a ³/₄" black ball. Attach it to the yellow end. Roll two yellow balls and attach for eyes. Flatten two small black balls and attach for pupils.

3 Wings: Flatten two ³/₄" long black ovals. Pinch the ends together. Attach where the body joins the head. Spread the tops apart. **Legs**: Roll six 1" long black teardrops. Curve each into an S. Attach the round ends of three legs evenly spaced on each side.

HEDY HOPPER

Model Magic®: green, yellow, black
basic supplies (see inside the front cover)

1 Body: Shape a 2" long green oval. Flatten a ¹/₂" green ball and press onto one end. **Head**: Roll a 1" ball and attach to the flat end. Use your little finger to indent the top front. Attach two ³/₈" yellow balls for eyes. Attach black balls for pupils.

2 Antennae: Roll two ³/₄" long green teardrops. Press the points together and attach between the eyes. Curve the round ends out and forward. **Wings**: Flatten two 1¹/₂" long yellow ovals. Flatten many small green balls all over both sides. Pinch the ends

together, then attach the joined end behind the joint of the body.

3 Back legs: Roll two 2¹/₂" long green teardrops. Bend as shown in the pattern. Attach one on each side of the body so the feet are even with the back end. **Front legs**: Roll two 1" long green teardrops. Attach the large ends on each side of the front body front segment. Curve the small ends under the head so it appears to rest on them. **Middle legs**: Roll two 1" long green teardrops. Attach the points under the body between the front and back legs. Curve the feet forward.

14

LADY ANN BUG

Model Magic®: black, red, white
basic supplies (see inside the front
  cover)

1 **Body**: Roll a 1¼" black ball. Flatten the bottom so it will sit. **Head**: Attach a ¾" black ball to the top. Use your thumb to indent for the eyes. **Eyes**: Roll two ⅜" black balls. Pinch the fronts to flatten them slightly, then attach with the thin sides to the front. Attach two white balls to the black pieces. Attach a red ball for her nose.

2 Flatten a ¾" tall red ball into a teardrop. Use the knife to indent the round end, making a  heart. Attach to her tummy as shown. **Arms**: Roll six 1" long black teardrops. Attach three evenly spaced on each side of the body (reinforce them with toothpick pieces). Curve the round ends forward—the top pair of arms should touch the heart.

3 **Wings**: Flatten a 1" red ball to 1½" across and cut in half. Trim a thin wedge off the top of each cut edge,  then press the trimmed edges together. Cut a curve away from the top so the wings will fit under the back of her head. Flatten several black

back view

balls on the wings for spots. Attach the wings to her back. After the ladybug is dry, use the black pen to draw pupils in her eyes.

wings

DARWIN DOODLEBUG

Model Magic®: green, yellow, red, white
basic supplies (see inside the front cover)

1 **Body**: Roll two 1" balls, one yellow and one red. Flatten slightly and press together. **Head**: Roll a ¾" yellow ball and attach to the body top. Flatten many small red balls all over the head and lower body.

2 **Eyes**: Attach two ⅜" green balls to the top front of the head. Attach a small white ball to the center of each green ball. Attach a red ball for his nose. **Antennae**: Roll a ⅛"x1¼" red log. Bend into a V and attach the point between the backs of the eyes. Curve each antenna outward.

3 **Arms**: Roll six ¼"x¾" green ropes. Attach one to each bottom side of the body, one on each side of the center body joint and one on each side of the neck. Curve each forward. **Wings**: Flatten two ¾" green ovals, join at the ends, then attach to the top back of the body. Bend the wings apart.

back view

LEONARD LIZARD

Model Magic®: green, red, black
spoon
basic supplies (see inside the front cover)

1 **Body**: Roll a 6¹/₂" long green teardrop with the fattest part about 1¹/₂" from the round end. Curve the tail as shown. **Head**: Flatten a 1¹/₂" long green egg. Attach with the small end extending past the front. Use the knife to draw a smile.

2 **Spine**: Twist together a ¹/₄"x4" red rope and a ¹/₄"x4" green rope. Roll to ¹/₄" wide. Attach to the top of the body. Cut off any extra at the end. Pinch the top to a point.

3 **Eyes**: Roll two ¹/₂" green balls. Pinch between your thumb and forefinger so they are thinner on one side. Attach to the head with the thin edges on the outsides. Slightly flatten two red balls and attach to the green balls. Flatten two tiny black balls as thin as you can. Attach to the lower outsides of the red balls.

4 **Feet**: Roll two ¹/₂"x3" green ropes. Roll each a little thinner in the center. Use the tip of the spoon to cut half circles out of the ends for toes. Curve one pair in a U, flatten the center and attach under the body so the toes are even with the front. Flatten the center of the second pair and attach behind the first, curving them slightly forward. **Spots**: Flatten several red balls and attach to the sides.

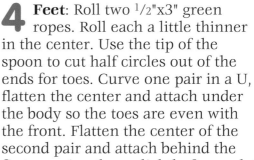
back view

SALLY MANDER

Model Magic®: red, yellow, black
basic supplies (see inside the front cover)

1 **Body**: Roll a 7" long red teardrop. Use your forefinger to roll the neck smaller. Curve the body and tail as shown. **Eyes**: Use your little finger to indent each side of the head. Attach a red ball to each side. Attach a smaller black ball to each red ball.

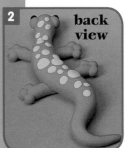
left side view

2 **Legs**: Roll a ¹/₂"x2¹/₄" red log and a ¹/₂"x2" red log. Flatten the centers. Press the shoulders onto the 2" log. A little farther back, press the body onto the 2¹/₄" log. Attach three little red balls to the end of each leg for toes. Flatten many little yellow balls all over her back.

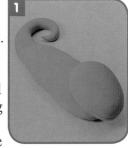
back view

SPEEDY SNAIL

Model Magic®: yellow, blue, white
basic supplies (see inside the front cover)

1 **Body**: Roll a 4¹/₂" long blue teardrop. **Shell**: Roll a ¹/₂"x8" yellow rope. Coil one end into a circle. Make another coil, slightly smaller, on top of the first. Continue to coil upward, forming a cone. Flatten an area of the body and attach the shell to it. Curve the head up along the front of the shell, then bend the round end forward.

2 **Eyes**: Attach two blue balls to the top of the head. Use your little finger to indent the fronts. Attach white balls in the indentions. **Antennae**: Roll two ¹/₈"x⁵/₈" yellow ropes. Pinch together at one end. Attach behind the eyes and curve them apart. After he's dry, use the black pen to draw his smile and the pupils of his eyes.

CAMI LEON

Model Magic®: yellow, orange, black
spoon
basic supplies (see inside the front cover)

1 **Body**: Roll an 8" long yellow teardrop with the fattest part about 2" from the round end. Coil the tail in a spiral as shown. Marble (see inside the front cover) yellow and orange clay together. All the remaining pieces except the black pupils will be made of the marbled clay. **Spine**: Roll a ¹/₄"x3" rope. Starting 1" from the large end, attach down the center of the back. Pinch to a point at the top.

2 **Eyes**: Slightly flatten two balls and attach to the top of the head, with half of each bending upward and touching the other eye. Roll two black balls and attach to the centers. **Mouth**: Roll a ¹/₈"x4" rope, fold it in half and pinch to flatten each end. Wrap around the face.

3 **Feet**: Roll two ¹/₂"x2" ropes. Use the tip of the spoon to cut half circles out of the ends for toes. Bend one pair of legs in a V. Attach to the body bottom so the toes are even with the lips. Curve the second pair and attach 1" behind the first. **Spots**: Flatten four balls on each side, evenly spaced.

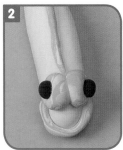

17

FRAZIER T. FROG

Model Magic®: red, yellow, black
basic supplies (see inside the front cover)

1 **Body**: Roll a 1¹/₂" long red egg and flatten slightly. Use the knife to draw a mouth on the large end. **Eyes**: Use your finger to indent each side of the top at the widest point. Attach a red ball in each indentation. Attach a black ball to each red ball, then a yellow ball on each black ball.

2 **Legs**: Roll two red dumbbells to match the small pattern. Attach the large ends on each side of the mouth. Bend the small ends forward. Roll two more to match the large pattern. Attach to the back sides and curve the legs as shown. Attach three red balls to the front of each foot for toes. **Spots**: Flatten several yellow balls onto the back and back legs.

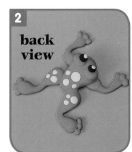

2 **back view**

SNAKE SEXTET

Model Magic®: red, black, white, your choice
basic supplies (see inside the front cover)

1 All snakes are made the same way—vary the lengths and thicknesses for different looks. **Body**: Marble (see inside the front cover) two or more colors. Roll into a long rope, then roll one end thinner for the tail. Coil the body in a spiral, S curves, hang the neck over the side of a shelf—or as you wish.

2 **Head**: Use the knife to cut a mouth in the round end. Open the mouth to be as fierce as you want. **Optional tongue**: Flatten a ¹/₈"x1" red rope and attach inside the mouth. Ripple the tongue where it comes out of the mouth. Leave the mouth wide open or close it partially over the tongue. **Eyes**: Place two white balls side by side on the top of the head. Press two smaller flattened black balls in the centers.

2

BECKY BUTTERFLY

Model Magic®: orange, blue, yellow
basic supplies (see inside the front cover)

1 **Wings**: Flatten two 1" long orange teardrops. Attach at the points with the rounded ends angled apart. Flatten two 1½" orange teardrops. Attach over the tops of the small teardrops, angling the points apart and slightly overlapping the rounded sides as shown in the pattern below. Roll many yellow balls and six blue balls. Flatten and attach as shown, making the left and right sides match.

2 **Body**: Shape a 1" long blue teardrop. Attach a ³/8" blue ball to the point of the teardrop. Attach a larger blue ball to the first ball. Attach the body to the wings. **Antennae**: Roll a skinny ³/4" long yellow rope and bend into a V. Curve the tips apart and attach the point to the top of the head. After the butterfly is dry, use the pen to dot her eyes and draw her smile.

KATEY PILLAR

Model Magic®: yellow, green, orange, black
basic supplies (see inside the front cover)

1 **Body**: Roll five ³/8"–³/4" yellow balls. Attach in a row in size order. Roll a ³/4" yellow ball and attach to the top of the large end, slightly to the front, for a head. Roll a ¹/2" long green cone and attach for a tail, curving the tip up. Flatten many green balls and attach randomly all over the top of the body.

2 **Eyes**: Roll two green balls. Attach to the top of the head. Use your little finger to indent the tops. Flatten two yellow balls in the indentions. Flatten two tiny black balls onto the tops of the yellow balls. **Nose**: Roll an orange oval and attach under the eyes.

back view

FIREHEART

Model Magic®: green, white, red, orange
ball-headed pin (to indent nostrils)
basic supplies (see inside the front cover)

1 **Body**: Roll a 5" long green teardrop. Press down to flatten the bottom. Tip the tail up. Flatten a 1" green ball on the front for his chest. Flatten a $3/4$" green ball on top of the chest for his neck.

2 **Head**: Roll a $1^1/4$" and a $3/4$" long green oval. Flatten one end of each. Attach the small to the large for a chin. Pull the lip down. Attach the head to the neck. Use the pin head to indent the nostrils.

3 **Eyes**: Attach two green balls on top of the head. Press white balls into the fronts.
Flames: Marble (see inside the front cover) orange and red. Flatten four $1/4$"x1" ropes, pinch together at one end and insert into the mouth. Bend the ends apart.

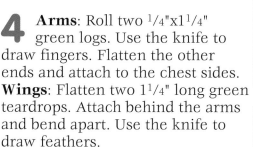

4 **Arms**: Roll two $1/4$"x$1^1/4$" green logs. Use the knife to draw fingers. Flatten the other ends and attach to the chest sides.
Wings: Flatten two $1^1/4$" long green teardrops. Attach behind the arms and bend apart. Use the knife to draw feathers.

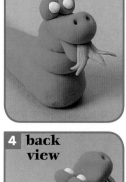
back view

5 **Ears**: Make like the wings, but use $1/2$" teardrops. Attach behind the eyes. **Scales**: Flatten many green balls. Overlap like roof shingles on the back, with the smallest near the tail. Flatten a few red balls down each side. **Spikes**: Flatten nine $3/8$" tall green cones. Attach to the back, with one on the back of the chest. **Feet**: Roll three $1/4$"x$3^1/4$" green ropes. Pinch together at the centers and attach under the body. After he's dry, use a pen to draw pupils in his eyes.

STEGGIE SAURUS

Model Magic®: blue, white, black
basic supplies (see inside the front cover)

1 **Body**: Roll a 5" long blue teardrop. Roll behind the large end with your finger to form a neck and head. Use your finger to indent twice on each side of the body for the legs. Use the knife to draw a mouth. **Eyes**: Attach two white balls to the top of the head. Flatten two tiny black balls and attach to the fronts.

2 **Legs**: Roll four $3/4$" tall blue cones. Flatten the top of each into a body indent. **Spikes**: Roll seven $1/4$"–$1/2$" tall cones. Curve the two smallest and attach to the tip of the tail, one in front of the other. Flatten the rest and attach as shown, with the tallest at the top of the back.

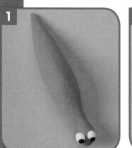
back view

back view

TRICER O'TOPS

Model Magic®: orange, white, black
basic supplies (see inside the front cover)

1 **Body**: Roll a 3³/₄" long orange teardrop. Use your finger to indent twice on each bottom side for the legs.
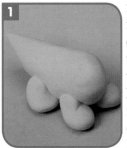
Legs: Roll four 1" tall orange cones. Flatten the top of each into a body indent. Pinch the bottoms of the front legs into toes.

2 **Ruff**: Flatten a 1¹/₂" orange ball to 2" across.

Attach to the body front, angled slightly backward. Use the knife to draw lines around the top half.
Head: Shape a 1¹/₄" long orange cone. Attach to the center of the ruff. Bend the point up. Use the knife to draw a mouth.

3 **Horns**: Roll three ⁵/₈" tall orange cones. Attach one to the nose tip and two to the back of the head.

back view
Eyes: Attach an orange ball in front of each back horn. Use your little finger to indent the fronts. Attach a white ball in each indentation. Flatten two black balls onto the fronts of the white balls for pupils.

BRONTY SAURUS

Model Magic®: green, white, black
basic supplies (see inside the front cover)

1 **Body**: Roll a 6" long green oval, then keep rolling one end into a long pointed tail. 2" from the round end, press with your fingers and roll to form a long neck and round head. The body will now be about 10" long. Use the knife to draw a mouth. Curve the tail forward. Bend the neck in an S so the head is above the front of the body. Use your finger to indent twice on each bottom side of the body for the legs.

2 **Eyes**: Slightly flatten two ³/₈" green balls and attach to the top of the head. Slightly flatten two white balls into the fronts of the green balls. Attach black balls to the fronts of the white balls.

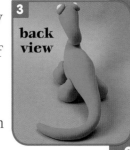
back view

3 **Legs**: Shape four 1¹/₄" tall green cones. Flatten the small end of a cone into each indentation.

DRAGGIN' DOGGY

Model Magic®: blue, black, white, yellow, pink (red + white)
basic supplies (see inside the front cover)

1 **Car**: Shape a 1½"x2½" blue rounded rectangle. Flatten the bottom. Use your thumb to hollow out a cockpit. Flatten four ⅞" black balls for wheels. Flatten a blue ball into the center of each wheel and a small black ball on each blue ball. Attach the wheels so they extend ¼" below the car. Flatten a 1" wide blue oval and attach to the back for a trunk. Curve a ⅛"x½" white log and attach the ends to the lid for a handle.

2 Flatten two ½" white balls and attach for headlights. Attach yellow balls to the fronts. Use the knife to draw crisscross lines. Attach a ¼"x1½" blue rope under the headlights for a bumper. Form a ¼"x2¼" black rope into a circle. Attach for a steering wheel.

3 **Dog**: Place a ¾" white ball in the cockpit. Attach another for the head. Attach two small white balls to the face for the muzzle. Attach a black ball for the nose and a ¼" pink oval for his tongue, curling the tip up. Flatten two 1" long black ovals. Attach for ears, shaping as if they were flying in the wind. Shape two 1" long white teardrops. Attach the points to his shoulders and the round ends to the steering wheel. After he's dry, use a pen to dot his eyes and whiskers.

BUMPER BUNNY

Model Magic®: pink (red + white),
blue, white, black
basic supplies (see inside the front
cover)

1 **Car**: Follow steps 1–2 for the Draggin' Doggy car, but use the colors shown in these photos. The wheels are plain black, and the steering wheel is made like the wheels except it's blue. Shape a ½" long blue oval for the trunk handle. Don't draw lines on the headlights. Leave out the bumper.

2 Flatten a ¾" blue ball to 1" wide. Attach to the inside back of the cockpit for a seat. **Bunny**: Place a ⅝" white ball in the cockpit. Attach a ¾" white ball for the head. Flatten two small white balls onto the face for the muzzle. Attach a pink ball for the nose.

3 Flatten two 1" long white ovals. Attach for ears. Shape two ¾" long white teardrops. Attach the points to the shoulders and the round ends to the steering wheel.

4 **Sunglasses**: Flatten a black ball on a ⅜" blue ball. Repeat. Attach above the nose. Roll two ⅛"x¾" blue ropes. Attach one to each side of the glasses. Press them along the sides of the head, curving the ends down.

ROBOTO

Model Magic®: orange, blue, black
basic supplies (see inside the front cover)

1 **Legs**: Flatten two ³/₄" black balls side by side. Stack flattened orange and blue balls on top as shown. **Body**: Attach a 1¹/₂" orange square, ¹/₂" thick.

2 **Arms**: Roll six blue and four orange ¹/₂" balls. Flatten and join as shown. Flatten two ¹/₂" black balls and cut a wedge out of each for hands. Attach the arms to the shoulders and the hands to the arms.

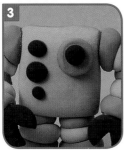

3 **Shirt decorations**: Flatten a small black ball in the center of a ¹/₂" blue ball for his badge. Flatten three small black balls and attach for the buttons.

4 **Head**: Flatten a ¹/₂" blue ball and attach to the body top. Shape a 1" blue square, ¹/₂" thick, and put on top.

5 **Face**: Use ³/₈" orange balls for eyes and little black balls for pupils. Make a black triangle for the nose. Roll an orange oval for his mouth.

6 **Ears**: Flatten an orange ball on each side of the head. Attach little blue balls to the centers. **Hat**: Flatten a ³/₈" orange ball, a ¹/₄" blue ball and a smaller orange ball. Stack on top of the head. Put a small black ball on top.

GZNK THE MARTIAN

Model Magic®: green, blue, yellow, black
ball-headed pin (to indent the nose)
basic supplies (see inside the front cover)

1 **Legs**: Flatten two ⁵/₈" yellow balls. Stack flattened blue and yellow balls on top. **Body**: Flatten four 1¹/₄"–³/₄" green balls. Stack on the legs as shown. **Arms**: Attach a ¹/₄"x1¹/₂" blue rope to each side. Attach blue balls for hands. Curve the arms forward and put the hands on his tummy.

2 **Head**: Attach a 1" blue ball to the top. Flatten four ¹/₈"–³/₈" green balls and stack in size order for his nose. Indent the end with the pin head. Attach yellow balls for eyes. Flatten a tiny black ball in the center of each eye. Flatten two ³/₈" green balls into teardrops. Attach to the head as shown for ears.

3 **Hat**: Flatten five ¹/₈"–³/₈" yellow balls. Stack in size order on his head. Place a ¹/₈" blue ball on top. **Hoses**: Curve two ¹/₄"x1¹/₄" yellow ropes. Attach the ends to his back.

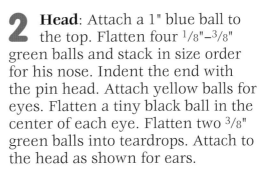

back view

back view

LOLLIPOP

Model Magic®: red, white
9" of 1/4" wide green satin ribbon
craft stick
7" of metallic gold cord or thread
basic supplies (see inside the front cover)

1 Follow step 1 for the candy cane, but roll the rope thinner and coil into a spiral. Let dry.

2 Knot the cord ends together. Glue the knot to one end of the craft stick, then glue the stick to the bottom back of the spiral so the knot is between them. Tie the ribbon into a bow and glue as shown.

SANTA CLAUS

Model Magic®: red, white, black, pink (red + white)
basic supplies (see inside the front cover)

CANDY CANE

Model Magic®: red, white, green
basic supplies (see inside the front cover)

1 Roll a 1/2"x6" white rope and a 1/2"x6" red rope. Twist together (see inside the front cover). Roll on a hard surface until they form a smooth striped rope. Bend into a candy cane and trim off the ends.

2 Flatten two 1/2" green balls into diamonds. Use the knife to draw vein lines. Attach to the cane as shown. Roll three 1/4" red balls and attach in a cluster over the leaves.

leaf

1 **Feet**: Roll two 7/8" black balls into ovals and flatten one end. Attach the thin ends side by side, toes out. **Body**: Roll a 1 5/8" red ball and place on the feet. Roll a 1 1/8" red ball and place on the first one.

mitten

2 **Arms**: Shape two 7/8" red balls into teardrops. Attach the small ends to the shoulders. Pull one arm down around his tummy. Bend the other up into a wave. Flatten two 1/2" white balls into ovals. Indent one side of each with the knife to make mittens. Attach one to the end of each arm. **Head**: Roll a 1" pink ball and attach to the body top. **Hat**: Flatten a 3/4" white ball and place on top of the head.

3 Roll a 4" long red cone. Attach to the center of the white and curve over the shoulder as shown. **Beard**: Roll a 3" long white cone. Attach to his chin and curve onto his chest. **Mustache**: Shape a 1/2" white ball into a cone and flatten. Use the knife to draw hair lines. Attach above the beard. Roll a red nose and attach above the mustache. After he's dry, use the pen to dot his eyes.

back view